HEALING - THE SHAMAN'S WAY
BOOK 5 - USING VIBRATION TO HEAL

Norman W. Wilson PhD

HEALING - THE SHAMAN'S WAY
BOOK 5 - USING VIBRATION TO HEAL

Cover Design by
S.R. Walker Designs
www.srwalkerdesigns.com

Interior Design
Omar Lopez, PhD

ZADKIEL PUBLISHING

A ZADKIEL PUBLISHING PAPERBACK

© Copyright 2024
Norman W. Wilson PhD

The right of Norman W. Wilson to be identified as author and channel of this work has been asserted by him in accordance with the Copyright, Designs and Patents Act 1988.

All Rights Reserved

No reproduction, copy or transmission of the publication may be made without written permission.

No paragraph of this publication may be reproduced, copied or transmitted save with the written permission of the publisher, or in accordance with the provisions of the Copyright Act 1956 (as amended).

Any person who does any unauthorised act in relation to this publication may be liable to criminal prosecution and civil claims for damages.

ISBN: 978-1-78695-873-0

Zadkiel Publishing
An Imprint of Fiction4All
www.fiction4all.com

This Edition
Published 2024

DISCLAIMER

Evidence supporting the use of various vibrations for healing purposes is growing but considerably more research is required. As with other supportive medicine modalities, there is ample testimonials supporting the use of sound vibrations. Yet, to claim sound vibrations work as healing tools may be no more than the result of the placebo effect. My attitude is "So what! If it makes you feel better, use it." As with any of the supportive medicines, always check with your medical doctor before using them.

A SPECIAL THANKS TO

Stuart Holland, my publisher, for his advice and personal completion of this work, and in bringing it to the printed page.

Stephen R. Walker, my book cover designer, for his personal attention to the execution of design appropriate for the subject matter of this book.

Omar Lopez, Ph.D. for his keen insights in creating the interior design of this book.

Suzanne V Wilson, my wife, who is always there for me.

ONE
SOUNDING OFF

To say vibration is everywhere is very much an understatement. It is the essence of all that is. It is the *all* of existence. There is nothing in this world that does not vibrate. In fact, the Cosmos itself, vibrates. The focus here is the deliberate use of vibration to create healing sounds—sounds to heal the physical, the mental, and the emotional aspects of the body. Please keep in mind that the use of the word body does not exclusively apply to just the human body. All bodies are included: human, animal, plant, or something from the aether.

The vibration holding central interest here is sound. Eileen Day McKusick defines sound as the *transmitted vibration of any frequency*[i] Sound as an instrument of healing has been around for thousands of years. Some estimates indicate sound used for healing dates back at least 40,000 years.

Healers of Ancient Egypt used chanting to treat illness. Early Tibetans used 'singing bowls, and healers of Native American tribes believed certain sounds were good for healing the sick. Yogis in Ancient India used sound to calm the mind, thus lowering stress levels. Pythagoras, the Greek philosopher, prescribed music as medicine. Known as the "father of music," he used harmonic frequencies to induce healing.

In 1839, Heinrich Wilhelm Dove discovered the neurological effect of binaural beats. In the mid-twentieth century, Sir Peter Guy Mannes, an English osteopath developed a machine to produce therapeutic sound vibrations to heal cells in the body. In 1977, Fabien Maman shaped the use of tuning forks for sound therapy. In 1996, the use of sound had begun to come into its own with the creation of the UK Sound Healers Association by Simon Heather.

Today, vibration has become a top choice in physical, mental, and emotional healing modalities. Sound baths, gongs, drums, crystal bowls, flutes, bells, tuning forks as well as chanting are now considered standard tools of vibrational treatment. If you stop and listen you will note the natural world is a euphony of vibration.

What is Vibration Therapy? Danielle Dixon has stated "Vibration Therapy is a holistic approach that uses vibration to improve well-being and promote healing. Vibration waves are delivered through the body via a vibration plate or machine."[ii] Sports medicine and its partner, pain management have advanced the use of vibration as a healing modality. A partial list of medical conditions that respond to vibrational treatment include the following:

Muscle Pain	Knee injury	Muscle atrophy
Sciatica	Back pain	Bone loss
Blood Pressure	Stress	Fibromyalgia
Urinary issues	Circulation	Restless Leg

Vibrational and sound therapy can have negative side effects. These include the following: Dizziness, Headaches, Numbness in the limbs, Injuries caused by the over use of a machine, back pain increased or developed, and conflicts with current or emotional issues.

In the medical field there are generally two types of vibration therapy that receive attention: Whole-body Vibration Therapy during which the client sits or lies on a vibrating platform and Focal Vibration Therapy targets specific areas of the body.

However, a third Vibration Therapy treatment is gaining approval, recognition, and use. This is Vibrational Sound Therapy, a primary focus of this book.

There are other devices besides vibration plates and machines. Sound is the operative word.

The current dominant theory behind sound healing is Brainwave Entrainment. It is also referred to as Brainwave Synchronization and or Neural Entrainment. According to Wikipedia, Brainwave Entrainment is that large-scale electrical oscillations in the brain will naturally synchronize to the rhythm of periodic external stimuli. That's a mouthful. Simply put, Brainwave Entrainment is a technique that uses rhythmic auditory or visual stimuli to guide the brainwaves into a desired state.

There are several types of Brainwave Entrainment stimuli available. Three sound-based stimuli include the following:

Monaural beats which are two different tones played at slightly different frequencies. A pulsing sound is perceived and are good for bringing about relaxation and sleep.

Binaural beats are two identical tones played at slightly different frequencies. But, one tone is played louder in one ear than in both. This creates the impression that beat frequency is coming from the center of the head. Binaural beats are often used to create specific brainwave states, such as alpha or beta waves.

Isochronic tones are pure tones that are pulsed on and off at a specific frequency. They are used to induce meditation and creativity.

Despite the fact the current use of Brainwave Entrainment is relatively new to modern medical healing techniques, there is evidence suggesting it may be beneficial in treating the following conditions: Anxiety, Depression, Pain, Sleep Issues, Focus and Concentration.

Brainwave Entrainment is not a cure-all nor is it a substitute for modern medical treatment. It is not a game. It can cause seizures, dizziness, headaches, and nausea. Women who are pregnant should mostly likely avoid using Brainwave Entrainment

It is important to start Brainwave Entrainment with short periods of time—five to ten minutes for several session. Gradually increase the length of time.

To get accustomed to using sound to heal try the following activity.

ACTIVITY ONE:

USING YOUR VOICE TO CREATE A RELAXED STATE

Directions:

Sit in a comfortable chair. Turn the lights down low or if you are doing this during the day, lower the window blinds to reduce the amount of light in the room.

Relax your facial muscles. Open and close your mouth several times to release any intention in your jaws. Take a deep yawn.

Inhale a deep breath through your nose.

Barely open your lips.

Slowly exhale through your parted lips. As you do, begin to hum until the exhale is completed. Do not change the tone or pitch of your voice.

Do this for about five minutes.

When finished, sit quietly for a few minutes. Notice any change in your feelings.

Practice this every day for one week. Select a specific time for each day: Just before you get up in the morning or as you bed down for the night.

It has been established that different conscious states can be associated with different brainwave frequencies. Research has shown, for instance, that acoustic entrainment of delta waves during sleep had a functional effect of memory improvement in healthy individuals. The nature of the issue determines the vibrational frequencies to be used. For example, 285Hz is helpful for the healing of wounds and tissue regeneration. Hz is from the last name of the physicists Heinrich Hertz. It refers to the number of cycles per second that an oscillation occurs.

Certain regions of the brain respond to different sounds and because the brain is impacted by sound vibrations, it reflects those vibrations.

The claimed benefits of vibrational healing techniques include the following: Calmness, positive outlook, less pain, being more aware, feeling less stress, having less fatigue, more mental energy, more physical energy, a greater sense of inner peace, increased memory, better sleep, better join functions, less headaches, deeper meditation, and concentration.

Nearly anything that can be used to make sound is a potential instrument for vibrational healing. Among the traditional instruments are the following: Tibetan Singing Bowls, Tuning Forks, Gongs, Drums, Flutes, Rattles, Tibetan Bells, and of course, the human voice.

As with sound creating instruments, there are several types of healing sessions that may last from 45 minutes to 90 minutes depending on the nature of the issue.

Typical sessions may include sound baths, guided visualizations with sound, chanting, vibroacoustics, Acutonics, and binaural beats.

Sound healing may be transmitted to human beings in the following ways:

The individual's voice as demonstrated in the earlier activity

The individual's voice is joined by other voices.

The individual voice is used while listening to music.

The individual voice is used while listening to a specific instrument, and the individual voice

is used in conjunction with a recording.

One of the earliest sounds is that of OM or as it is sometimes spelled; AUM. OM is filled with a 5000-year-old history from the Vedic Texts of Ancient India. Its mysticism includes the symbolism of the Universe's origin as well as the sound of creation. Symbolically, it means the truth of ultimate reality. Additionally, it represents the oneness of all that is and the connection to the Universe.

Considered to be one of the most significant and important symbols, OM is closely aligned will all that is Spiritual.

OM's number 3 shaped construction connects many of the 3 symbols so prominent in Eastern belief systems.

Science research has found that OM when chanted activates the Vagus Nerve, the largest never in the human body. The Vagus Nerve helps regulate the parasympathetic nervous system which controls the heart rate, blood pressure, and your mood. Research has also shown that the repetition of OM for just a few minutes a day reduces anxiety, stress, and depression.

ACTIVITY TWO

ACCEPTING THE GIFT OF OM[iii]

Directions:

Choose a quiet place (not in bed),

Burn an incense. Lavender works nicely or use a personal favorite),

Sit in a comfortable chair,

Dim the lights,

Take 5 deep breaths, exhaling with some force,

sing or hum OM,

Do this for 10 to 15 minutes

Do this daily if you can arrange it. If not, sing OM at least 3 times weekly

TWO
PLAYING AROUND:

Humankind has long played with sounds. This has been especially true of its healing and spiritual endeavors. Many of the early religions and traditions speak of the world being created by sound:

The Ancient Egyptians believed Thoth created the universe with his voice

In Zoroastrianism, *Ahura Mazda's* First Thought produced The

"Bang" or Sound or Resonance of the Divine Word *"Ahunavar,"* resulting in the manifestation of the universe

The Hopi Indians believed the inanimate forms on Earth were brought to life by Spider Woman who sand the *Song of Creation*

Australia's Indigenous People believed the sound of the didgeridoo was responsible for the creation of the world

Polynesians believed the gods blew conch shells to create the world.

The point here is that sound (vibration) has always been a part of human existence. The primary focus is for you to experience some of the voices of sound and that means your participation. The activities are designed to give you an arsenal of self-help.

ACTIVITY THREE

AY HEY YO

The purpose of this activity is to increase the flow of oxygen into the lungs. If you are experiencing breathing issues caused by COVID-19, COPD, Pneumonia, or Asthma continual use of this activity will help ease your breathing. If you have issues be sure you check with your medical doctor before attempting this exercise.

Directions:

Assume the Lotus Pose or sit in a comfortable chair.

Inhale two deep breaths. Hold for the count of 5. Exhale for the count of five. Do this three times.

Say the following out loud: AY HEY YO three times. Sing-song it.

Lower your voice and say AY HEY HO three more times

Raise the pitch of your voice and say AY HEY YOU three more times.

Say or sing AY HEY YO whenever you feel tired or frustrated.

What is circulation in the human body? The circulatory system carries oxygen, and nutrients to cells, and removes waste products, like carbon dioxide. Arteries and veins are two of the body's main types of blood vessels. Arteries are blood vessels that carry oxygen-rich blood away from the heart to the body. Veins are blood vessels that carry blood that is low in oxygen from the body back to the heart for reoxygenation. All too often as we become engrossed in our activities, we tend to not breathe correctly.

ACTIVITY FOUR

CLAP YOUR HANDS, STOMP YOUR FEET[iv]

Directions:

Begin by slowly clapping your hands together. Gradually increase the speed. DO NOT clap so hard or fast as to injury your hands.

Stop clapping. Begin stamping your feet. Gradually increase the number of times you stamp.

Clap and stamp your feet at the same time. Set a comfortable pace.

Do this for 5 to 10 minutes.

DEALING WITH HEADACHES

A headache is a pain in the head or neck caused by irritation of the pain-sensitive structures in the head. The head and neck have many pain-sensitive structures, including blood vessels, muscles, nerves, and connective tissues.

There are many possible causes of headaches. Some of the most common causes include:

Tension headaches: These are the most common type of headache, and they are often caused by stress, muscle tension, or poor posture. Tension headaches typically cause a dull, aching pain on both sides of the head.

Migraine headaches: These are less common than tension headaches, but they can be more severe. Migraine headaches are often accompanied by other symptoms, such as nausea, vomiting, and sensitivity to light and sound.

Sinus headaches: These are caused by inflammation or infection of the sinuses, which are air-filled cavities in the bones of the face. Sinus headaches typically cause a dull, aching pain in the forehead, cheeks, or around the eyes.

Cluster headaches: These are a rare type of headache that causes severe pain on one side of the head. Cluster headaches typically occur in groups or clusters, and they can be accompanied by other symptoms, such as restlessness, tearing, and a runny nose.

Medication overuse headaches: These can occur when people overuse pain medication, such as over-the-counter pain relievers or prescription opioids. Medication overuse headaches can make headaches worse.

Withdrawal headaches: These are caused by the sudden stoppage of regular use of drinks and or food: coffee, alcohol, sugars.

ACTIVITY 5

This activity is a good one if you are inclined to limit the number of over-the-counter drugs or if you want to provide extra support for your prescribed treatment.

<u>Directions:</u>

Get comfortable.

Take the first two fingers of each hand and very gently tap your temples.

Slowly move the tapping across your forehead.

Do this for about three minutes. Do not apply pressure.

Do this as you begin to register a headache.

This is a modification of the Emotional Freedom Technique created by Gary Craig in the 1990s.

HAND PAIN AND WHAT YOU CAN DO ABOUT IT

Our hands are not only complex but are also delicate physical appendages that are composed of 27 bones. Unfortunately, there are many causes and specific types of hand pain. Bones, joints, connective tissues, tendons, and nerves can all be a point of pain. There are three major types of bones in the human hand: Phalanges, Metacarpal bones, and Carpal bones. Within these three types of bones are 27 smaller bones any one of which can have issues that cause pain.

Not only can there be pain in the bones of the hand there can be pain in the joints, connective tissues, tendons, and nerves. Hand pain can come from inflammation, nerve damage, repetitive motion injury, sprains, fractures, or from any one of several chronic health conditions. Among these chronic health issues are:

Arthritis, the inflammation of one or more joints, is the leading cause of hand pain. There are more than 100 types of arthritis; the most common being osteoarthritis.

Carpal Tunnel Syndrome occurs when the median nerve gets squeezed by a narrowing carpal tunnel. The associated pain includes burning, tingling, itching around the thumb, index finger, middle finger and or palm of the hand.

De Quervain's Tenosynovitis affects the tendons around the thumb. There might be pain around the thumb-side of the wrist, swelling near the base of the thumb, or a popping when the thumb is moved.

Ganglion Cysts around the wrist and hand are generally not painful. However, if there is significant fluid buildup pain could result

Gout is a form of arthritis and is very painful. Gout generally impacts the joint at the base of the big toe. It can occur in the hands.

Lupus, an autoimmune disease, causes joint pain and swelling of the hands, and wrists.

Peripheral neuropathy causes numbness, pain, and weakness in the hands and feet. It can be caused by nerve damage, diabetes, infections, and metabolic issues.

Raynaud's Phenomenon causes numbness and cold in the fingers and toes which may result in the loss of comfortable use of the hands and problems in walking.

Traumatic Injury is a very common hand injury. The hands are exposed to a large variety of dangers that are work and play related. Remember, there are 27 small bones in each hand and these can be broken in several different ways.

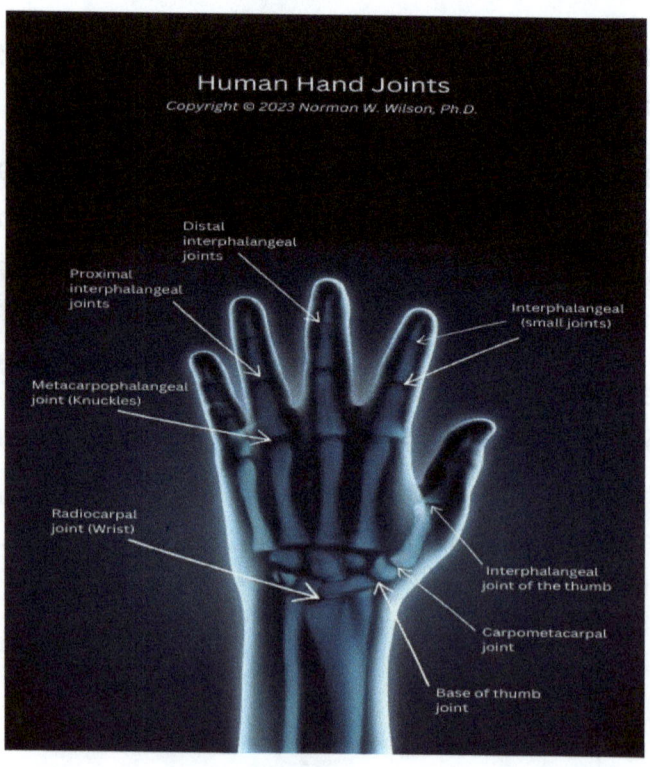

ACTIVITY 6: HANDS PAIN RELIEF

Here are several quick and easy things you can do to provide temporary relief from painful hands.

If your hands are hurting from too long sessions at the keyboard, playing a musical instrument, or any other continuous repetitive work, gently and GENTLY is the operative word, tap your fingers on your desk or table. Do this for no longer than 2 or 3 minutes. Then apply over-the-counter pain relievers or a prescription.

Gently rub your hands together until you feel them warm.

Clap your hands for a couple of minutes. Not hard.

THREE
LET IT GO

All human beings as well as animals experience stress. What is stress? It is a state of worry or mental tension, and or anguish created by difficult situations. It is both a psychological and physiological reaction to that which is a threat or challenge. From a psychological viewpoint, there are three main types of stress.

Acute Stress may be caused by bodily reactions to different situations that are not in the normal range of one's behaviors. These include job pressures, family issues, nagging aches and pains. Generally, and fortunately, Acute Stress is not long term.

Episodical Acute Stress comes about when one frequently experiences Acute Stress. Sufferers of EAS are health care professionals, EMS, police, firemen, and teachers.

Chronic Stress involves long periods of time. Often, those who experience and live continual stressful lives feel there is no way out; and that there is no chance of improvement.

There are different approaches that can be used to fight stress. The following 4 approaches have popular appeal:

Physical exercise on a regular basis, that is at least 3 times per week. The key here is to be consistent. Each exercise session should last at least 30 minutes. DON'T let the suggested time create more stress. Do what you can. Be consistent,

Meditation is on nearly every list of activities to do to reduce stress. There are at least 16 types of Meditation. I recommend *Mindfulness Meditation*. It is the process of being fully present with your awareness. Being mindful means being aware of where you are and what you are doing. It means not developing a thought or image but allowing it to move on—to let go.

Therapy as an approach to stress involves working with a life coach, psychologist, stress management specialist, or a spiritual counselor. This may involve several private sessions.

Vibration Therapy commonly referred to as *whole-body vibration* (WBV) requires a machine and a specialist. A vibrating machine, generally a platform on which one stands or sits. A therapist will determine position, speed, and length of time on the platform. These platforms are now available for home use. Be sure to check with your medical doctor before beginning such a therapy.

Sound Vibration involves the use of various instruments. These include drums, tuning forks, rattles, and recordings of sounds in nature, Binaural Beats, crystal bowls, and Tibetan Bowls.

ACTIVITY 7:

DOING IT YOUR WAY

<u>Directions:</u>

You will need two spoons, or two pencils, or Chinese Chopsticks.

Sit at your desk or at a table.

Gently begin to tap the objects of choice on the desk top or table.

Set an easy rhythm

Do this for about 10 minutes

ACTIVITY 8:

TUNING IN

Directions:

You will need a tuning fork. Tuning forks are preprogramed for specific musical notes. Select a tuning fork whose sound matches your need.

Tap the fork on a hard surface such as a rubber mallet.

Place the handle of the fork on bottom of your wrist.

Do this for 5 minutes and then switch wrists.

FOUR
GETTING THE BEAT ON FOR HEALING

Daily life is full of noise. It is true all noises are sound, but not all sounds are viewed as noise. Sound and noise are often interchanged, but there are several main differences. Things get a bit personal at this point. Accept the premise that sound for one person may be noise for another. Sound is any vibration that travels through a medium and can be perceived by one's ears. A medium is air, water, or certain solids. Noise is, on the other hand, unwanted or unpleasant sound. Noise implies a negative connotation—a disruption or annoyance that is loud, repetitive, and lacking organization. Think about the sounds you are bombarded with every waking hour of every day. Think about those in your home, workplace, on the street, in your car, or shopping center. Sound can have a purpose such as communicating or entertainment or as in this case, healing. Their intensity is measured in terms of decibels. A decibel is a logarithmic unit that is used to measure sound levels. The chart,

Everyday Creators of Noise and Their Decibels, lists a very small number of things you experience daily that creates noise.

EVERYDAY CREATORS OF NOISE AND THEIR DECIBELS

Noise Source	Decibels
Air Conditioner	50-75
Airplane	140
Alarm Clock	65-80
Ambulance Siren	120
Baby Crying	110
Blender	80-90
Boom Box	100
Coffee pot	55
Dishwasher	55-70
Electric Shaver	50-80
Electric Drill	95
Garbage Disposal	70-95
Handgun	166-170
Leaf Blower	110
Motorcycle	95-110
Rock Concert	110-120
Television	70
Vacuum Cleaner	60-85

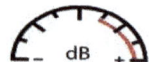

Copyright © 2023 Norman W. Wilson, Ph.D.

When combined, this noise is an unwelcome symphony that creates a variety of physical, mental, and emotional issues—everything from headaches, stomachaches, blurred vision, diarrhea, weight issues, to sexual malcontent. Even the natural sounds of the natural world can rip the nervous system. Since this is all true, how then can I advocate sound for healing?

There is a huge difference between noise and healing sounds: One has purpose; the other does not. The motive is to help the body to relax so it can then heal itself. Enter colors of sound. A rainbow of colors is often experienced by individuals who are bathed in sound.

In the field of audio engineering, we learn that sounds can be categorized into different colors based on each's power spectrum density. This depends on the size of the sound wave and its frequency and the speed of its vibration per second appear with different textures. This is why each signal has its own identifying sound and color. Remember, there is a huge difference between noise and sound especially when the sound is used for healing purposes.

The chart on the following page shows the color of sounds and what their suggested impact of healing is.

Binaural Beats

 **DIFFERENT NOISE COLORS**

White Noise - Helps mask background noises that can disrupt sleep. Sounds like that "shhh" when the TV or radio is tuned to an unused frequency. It's a mixture of all the frequencies humans can hear.

Pink Noise -pink noise can mask various sounds and unwanted background noise, it's the perfect choice for concentration. Many people who suffer from chronic tinnitus even note that pink noise has proven useful.

Brown/Red Noise - Activates, vitalizes, intensifies, releases blocked energy, and produces collagen.

Blue Noise - Reduces inflammation, produces restful sleep, and brings serenity and clarity.

Purple Noise - Has a high vibration level; is known for its effect on eyes, ears, nose, migraines, throat, lungs and sinuses.

Gray Noise - Used in the discipline of psycho-acoustics, to test people's hearing and to tackle insomnia, hyperacusis, and tinnitus..

Green Noise - Equalizes, relaxes, calms down, keeps physical and mental energy balanced. Can bring your heartbeat to normal and lower your stress hormone levels to help you sleep better.

Copyright © 2023 Norman W. Wilson, Ph.D.

Binaural Beats are not music nor are they sounds we normally hear. They are an auditory phenomenon created by the brain; that is, they are a perception of sound. Binaural Beats sound makes use of the physical fact that the right and left ear each receive sounds at slightly different frequency patterns or brain waves. It is generally recognized that there are five different frequency patterns or brain waves. The following diagram shows the five frequency patterns or brain waves with their associated Hertz.[v]

THE FIVE FREQUENCY PATTERNS
OR BRAIN WAVES

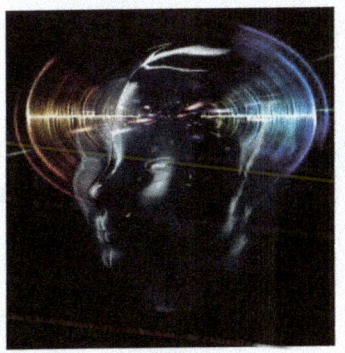

Frequency	Hertz
Alpha	7-13
Beta	12-30
Delta	0.5-4
Gamma	30-50
Theta	4-7

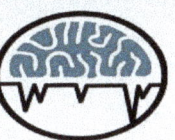

Copyright © 2023 Norman W. Wilson, Ph.D.

The question is how do you use Binaural Beats? First, you need a quality set of stereo headphones and an MP3 player. The player can be installed on your PC, iPad, or cellphone. Select a beat to help a specific issue. According to proponents of Binaural Beats, they help improve the following issues: Stress reduction, Anxiety, Improve self-confidence, Enhances deeper meditation, Improves psychomotor performance, and Uplifts one's mood.

Brain waves or brain patterns, as they are sometimes called, each have specific areas of influence. By that, it is meant specific areas of healing. Please note that this may vary from person to person.

Alpha Waves help you to relax and focus. They reduce stress and helps you maintain positive thinking and increases one's learning capabilities,

Beta Waves helps keep you focused, improves analytical thinking processes, stimulates your energy, and increases a higher level of cognition,

Delta Waves induces deep sleep, pain relief, improves meditation, cortisol reduction, and opens one's access to the unconscious mind,

Gamma Waves increase cognitive enhancement, helps memory recall, opens the way to thinking outside of the box, and

Theta Waves improves the depth of meditation, increases deep relaxation, and enhances creativity.

There may be negative side-effects to using Binaural Beats. For some individuals, Binaural Beats may increase the feeling of depression. Others may experience a deepened anxiety, an intensity in anger, or periods of confusion. Binaural Beats is NOT intended to replace modern medical practice. Always check with your doctor and schedule a follow-up appointment if you use Binaural Beats and feel any ill effects.

Solfeggio

Another type of sound that is widely used for healing is *Solfeggio*. According to *Dictionary. Com*, solfeggio is "a vocal exercise in which the sol-fa syllables are used. In this case, the musical scale in which the notes A through G have specific names. It has been claimed that the Solfeggio scale, originally a six-note, was developed by Guido d' Arezzo, a Benedictine monk in the 8th Century. Later, a seventh note was added and is currently used in music today.

Solfeggio Frequencies were primarily forgotten until the 20th Century. During the 1970s, a naturopathic physician, Dr. Joseph Puleo, rediscovered them. He used mathematical numeral reduction to identify six measurable tones that bring the body back into balance and aid in healing. It is believed these Solfeggio frequencies profoundly affect the conscious and subconscious mind. In1988, Dr. Glen Rein confirmed the impact of different music on human DNA. He exposed similar DNA to four kinds of music, each having different frequencies:

Gregorian chants, Sanskrit changes, Classical and Rock and Roll.

Dr. Rein, measured the rate of UV light absorption on DNA and was able to assess the effects of each type of music. The Gregorian and Sanskrit Chants had the most positive healing effects while Rock and Roll harmed the DNA.

Schumann Resonance

There is a reason why Solfeggio frequencies produce more positive effects on the body than other sounds. Physicist Winfried Otto Schumann in 1952 provided the answer. He found electromagnetic resonances existing between the earth's surface and the ionosphere and this resonance was at a low frequency—between 7.86 Hz and 8Hz. This resonance has since been called the Schumann Resonance.

Herbert Konig found that Schumann Resonances matched various levels of human brain activity. He compared EEG recordings with the Earth's electromagnetic fields. He found that this resonance matched the five different brain wave states: Delta, theta, alpha, beta, and gamma. We now have other research showing that the low frequency of the Schumann Resonance provides synchronization for higher brain functions.

Listening to Solfeggio Frequencies has its benefits. We begin with 852Hz.

852Hz helps the replacement of negative thoughts with those that are positive. One's inner strength and intuition may also receive a boost.

741Hz is an excellent frequency if you are struggling with living a healthy lifestyle It helps one's attempt to express themselves in a creative way.

639Hz helps balance emotions, elevate mood, and promotes open communication within interpersonal relationships.

396Hz helps remove subconscious fears, worries, and anxiety. It's especially good at helping one eliminate guilty feelings and that ugly underlying subconscious beliefs preventing you from personal achievement.

528Hz helps one heal and repair the physical body.[vi]

432Hz has an excellent calming effect. Opens the mind to feelings of peace and well-being.

Consider adding Binaural Beats and or Solfeggio listening time to your daily "take-care-of-yourself" routine. Here are some activities to help you heal yourself

ACTIVITY 9

Binaural Beats and Concentration

The lower range of Binaural Beats (14 to 30 Hz) are the beats that are generally said to improve concentration and over-all cognition. Play this in the morning after you have gotten up. Do this for 3 days, skip two and start the pattern over again. Then stop. Note any changes in concentration and cognition. The Internet has a large selection of Mp3 and Mp4 files available and they are free. Here is a YouTube presentation

https://www.youtube.com/watch?v=Wa9YSAdbKh8Then.

ACTIVITY 10

Rock-a-by Baby or Solfeggio Sleep

Listening to specific Solfeggio sounds can help you sleep better. Because 432 Hz is said to help fill the mind with feelings of peace and tranquility, it allows sleep to occur. Here is one URL for your use: https://www.youtube.com/watch?v=8s4Dhk3wZ60

Do this every night. Note how you feel when you get up in the morning. To help determine the effectiveness of the Solfeggio sound, skip two nights after the week's trial. If you feel restless, wakeful return to using the Solfeggio.

Mantras Healing

Using the vocal cords to heal comes from ancient cultures of several millennia ago. One of the popular ancient cultures is India's Hinduism. Its Vedic chants provide powerful sound-vibration healing tools for one's personal use or in a group setting.

With their specific sound vibrations created by specific syllabic rhythms create an energetic wave that resonates with the different parts of the human and animal bodies.

Chanting is one way to tune into the natural biological frequencies of the body. I add the physical brain and the emotional qualities generated by the mind. The centers of energy frequencies in Hinduism and Tibetan Buddhism are called *chakras*. Specific mantras are associated with specific chakras. Matching the mantra to a specific chakra helps insure greater healing potentiality.

Traditionally there are three types of mantras: Bija, meaning *seed,* Saguna meaning *with form*, and Nirguna, meaning *without form.* It is suggested that one repeat the mantra at least 108 times per session. There is some challenge to this number but as with everything in the world of healing, intention is the key to success. The most often noted and used include the following thee:

Om or Aum Mantra: This is the primordial sound, the connecting source

Gayatri Mantra: This is the vibration of unity, appreciation, and creation

Om Mani Padme Hum Mantra: This is the vibration of soothing, healing, and energizing.

What are the benefits of regularly using a mantra for healing? Among the benefits are the following:

Feeling good and as a result your self-esteem and self-confidence are improved.

Reduction of stress calms the mind, helps lower high blood pressure

Enhances personal spiritual awareness.

Promotion of sleep

Personal focus and concentration are improved.

ACTIVTY 11

Hum-humming Along

Directions:

Select one of the three mantras. Be sure it is one with which you feel comfortable.

Quietly repeat the mantra for 5 minutes.

Do this every morning immediately upon rising.

Say the mantra for 14 days.

FIVE
CRYSTALS THAT SHAKE YOU UP

Crystals have been defined as "solids that have an organized structure." Second, they have been identified as being homogeneous with a natural geometrically regular form. Additionally, this form has symmetrically arranged planes. Further, the way these planes are organized determines the stone. Crystals, like everything else vibrate.

It is said that earth vibrates at 7.83Hz while a human being vibrates between 5Hz and 8Hz; whereas, some crystals vibrate over 900Hz. The accepted high healing frequency is 174Hz. Pairing crystals with Solfeggio Frequencies adds another level of crystal-vibrational healing.

Be cautioned. You cannot hear the vibrations of crystals unless you have highly sophisticated equipment. However, you can feel it. The technical term for the way one acquires energies by touching crystals is *Piezoelectricity*. Clear Quarts Crystal is a good choice to begin to tune into the subtle vibrations of crystal healing energy.

ACTIVITY 12

Oh! Yes, I Can!

You Will Need:

One Clear Quartz Crystal about 2.54cm or a bit larger.

Six ounces of spring water or Lavender Hydrosol

One clean soft cloth for drying

Directions:

Warm the six ounces of spring water Lavender Hydrosol. Do not boil!

Place the crystal in the warmed water. Make sure the crystal is completely covered by the water. Leave the crystal in the water for 5 minutes.

After the five minutes, gently dry the crystal with the cloth.

Charge the crystal by placing it in the sun for 1 hour. In the event, it is a dark and cloudy day, place the crystal in a small bowl of sea salt. Leave it in the salt overnight.

If you used the sea salt, at the end of the time, remove the crystal and rinse it thoroughly with the spring water or hydrosol and carefully dry it.

Let the crystal rest for 30 minutes.

Place the Clear Quartz Crystal in the palm of your dominate hand. *Do not squeeze the crystal.* If you do, you only feel the pulse of your fingers.

Breathe softly. Be patient.

The sensation will be very subtle.

Practice for a few days if you did not feel the subtle vibration.

Since the focus here is vibrational healing, the question is there a healing crystal frequency takes center stage. Yes, there is. 14.7456mhz is viewed as the healing crystal frequency. (Check the following URL for what the 14.7455mhz sounds like.

https://www.youtube.com/watch?app=desktop&v=Z9HXa8Z5wIE).

According to a September 27th 2022 report by ChipSun, the 14.7456mbhz promotes the following seven benefits:

Effective in reducing anxiety, depression, and stress

Helps resolve addiction issues

Boosts the immune system

Uplifts one's attitude

Improves sleep

Develops one's spirituality

Improves cognitive function and memory recall

Specific uses can be assigned to crystals based on their Hertz. Hertz is important when combining crystals for a healing purpose. Each crystal no matter how small or how large has a distinct and unique vibration. It is that vibration that defines the energy blueprint. The mineral content of the crystal determines its vibration and that creates some crystals with higher vibration than others.

The following chart shows suggested crystals for specific use. The Hertz for each crystal is given.

CRYSTAL USE AND HERTZ CHART

USE	CRYSTAL	HERTZ
Relief	Selenite	174 Hz
Healing	Green Tourmaline	285 Hz
Liberation	Nuummite	396 Hz
Change	Tourmaline	417 Hz
Transformation	Lemurian	528 Hz
Relationships	Green Aventurine	639 Hz
Enlightenment	Azurite	741 Hz
Spirituality	Clear Apophyllite	852 Hz
Oneness	Clear Quartz	963 Hz

Copyright © 2023 Norman W. Wilson, Ph.D.

Before you get involved any further, remember to practice due diligence. Not all crystals are safe. They can cause physical, mental, or psychological issues—even death. It is a crystal's mineral content that is the harbinger of bad stuff. Some individuals may experience feeling dizzy, agitated, or nausea.

Probably all crystals can be combined. Admittedly, some combinations are particularly effective when done so for specific intentions. Nine crystals and their uses are listed in the "Crystal Use and Hertz Chart." Additional crystals and their use include the following:

To be more loving and to improve self-love: Ruby, Moonstone, Rose Quartz, Mangano Calcite, Amethyst, and Pink Tourmaline

To become more creative: Carnelian, Fire Agate, Citrine, Tiger's Eye, Orange Calcite, and Malachite

To be more grounded: Black Obsidian, Black Tourmaline, Hematite, Smokey Quartz, and Bloodstone

To deepen meditation: Danburite, Clear Quartz, Herkimer Diamond, Selenite, Moldavite, and Celestite

To aid sleep :Amethyst, Rose Quartz, Lepidolite, Blue Agate, Moonstone, and Clear Quartz

ACTIVITY 13

Bag It-Use it

<u>What You Will Need:</u>

A one-foot square of cloth (Your choice of type Silk, Cotton, Leather for example)

One pair of scissors

One sewing needle

Several inches of thread (Your choice of type and color)

Four or five crystals of your intention choice, that is to aid sleep, meditation, etc. The number depends on the size they are. Use more if the crystals are small.

Enough ribbon, leather rope, or string to tie the pouch together. The length of the ribbon will depend on the size of your neck or where you choose to hang it.

If you do not want to sew the cloth, you can use an appropriate glue for cloth. Stapels are not recommended because their metal may cause a disruption of the crystals' energy flow.

Directions:

Cut the cloth into a 4- or 6-inch square

Sew or glue 3 sides together. If you glue, be sure to leave enough time for it to dry before continuing to the next step.

Add the crystals

Sew in the ribbon, or simply tie it around the pouch.

Place the pouch under your pillow, lay it on a nightstand, wear it round your neck, tuck in a pocket, place it on your desk.

If you are a Reiki practitioner, consider using the following crystals with a client: Red Jasper, Blue Lace Agate, Bloodstone, Aquamarine, Rose Quartz, Orgonite, Rhodonite, Clear Quartz, Black Tourmaline, Tiger Eye, Amethyst, Shungite, Labradorite or Selenite.

SIX
DEALING WITH EMF

For hundreds of years, humans have recognized what is now called energy and its value. Ancient Chinese called this universal energy *qi.* In India, it is called *prana*. The Dogon of Africa called it *bayuali* and the Hopi Indians of the United States called it *kachina.* By whatever name this energy is called it is a life-force.

It is often said that everything vibrates even the stars and planets and have specific vibrating frequencies that are now recognized for their healing potentialities. Imagine bubbling ripples cascading flowing outward from a stone thrown into a pond. EMFs are similar in that they carry oscillating electric and magnetic fields of unseen waves.

This spectrum runs from a slow hum of power lines to the high-pitched hum of Wi-Fi. Each frequency and wavelength carry a unique energy signature. Sunlight, on the other hand, bathes the Earth in a low-frequency warmth; whereas, cell phones pulsate with high-frequency waves. Electric fields are created by differences in voltage. The higher the voltage the higher the resulting field.

Electromagnetic Fields (EMF) are everywhere in our environment. They *are* not visible *to the naked eye. Electric fields, f*or example, are created by a build-up of electric charges in the atmosphere resulting in lightning and thunderstorms.

The earth has a magnetic field. It causes the needle of a compass to point to the North. Birds as well as fish use Earth's magnetic field to navigate.

Besides the natural creation of EMF, there are those created by human beings: X-rays, television, radios, cellphones, computers, and all their subtypes. A chief characteristic of an electromagnetic field is its frequency or its corresponding wavelength. Obviously, constituents of the electromagnetic fields, including humans, react according to the different frequencies being experienced. For example, every electric socket in your home emits an electromagnetic field, albeit, at a low frequency.

An analogy will help. The following is a modified version provided by the World health Organization. Take a 6 to8 food rope 3/16 inches thick. Time one end to a door knob. Make sure its tight. Step back from the door the full length of the rope. Take the free end of the rope and slowly move the rope up and down. This will create one big wave. Move the rope up and down faster and a series of small waves will be created. Note, the length of the rope remains the same. However, the more waves you generate, the higher the frequency, the smaller will be the distance between them, that is, the shorter wavelength.

These invisible threads weave in and out of our modern lives, connecting nearly everything we do or use: appliances, power our communications, and eventually shape our reality. Magic is not involved. It is simply one of the many fantastic dances of our lives.

The signs that you have been overly exposed to Electromagnetism include the following: Constant aches and pains, High Blood Pressure, Weariness, Glucose level off, Headaches, Cholesterol changes, Sleeplessness, Nervousness, Cardiovascular issues, Low libido, Depression, and Memory loss.

Bear-in-mind, there may be other indicators of health issues such as those that are inherited, physical abuse, excessive alcohol use, and or high sugar consumption. Further, the World Health Organization's International Agency for Research on Cancer has reported Electromagnetic Fields are possibly carcinogenic to humans.

Knowing your EMF exposure starts with measuring it in your home. Use a pocket-sized gaussmeter to detect magnetic fields from appliances and home wiring. Gaussmeters costs $12 to $300 or more. The less expensive models work fine for home use. Remember, distance is your best friend when it comes to EMF exposure. EMF's intensity drops dramatically as you move away from the source.

ACTIVITY 14

 Making your own EMF Detector

What You Will Need:

One metal clothes hanger (no plastic coating)

One pair of wire cutters

One pair of scissors

One plastic straw

Directions:

Carefully cut the bottom of the hanger from the rest of it

Create a perfect letter L. One end should be longer than the other.

Cut a two-inch section from the plastic straw

Insert the bent end of the wire into the two-inch section of the straw

How to Use the EMF Detector:

Gently hold the end of the wire with the plastic straw between our thumb and forefinger. Do not squeeze.

Hold it an arm's length from your body. Your body energy will make it twirl around.

Go through each room in your home. The rod will swing back and forth whenever it detects energy. Fast swinging means high EMF energy. Slower means less.

In those areas in which a high level of EMF was detected, check the electrical outlets, plugs, lamps, and electric devices. If there is a very high EMF detected, you should call an electrician to check the outlets.

Devices should be checked for electrical issues.

Once you have determined there is an EMF issue in your home, home office, or kitchen, what can you do besides dumping your electronic devices?

Obviously, you are not going to get rid of coffee/teapots, toasters, microwaves, electric stoves, refrigerators, computers, cellphones, or your security system.

CRYSTALS AND EMF

Crystals have a long and varied history as stones of protection and in today's world, that includes the swamp of EMF that contaminates our space. It is unreasonable to suggest that all crystals neutralize the negativity of EMF. I recommend the following eight crystals to be used in wearable jewelry, placed on furniture in various places in your home or workplace. If jewelry is not an option carry a crystal on your person.

Black Tourmaline is considered one of the strongest protectors of all the crystals. It is excellent for diffusing the negative impact of EMF.

Citrine helps the body repair itself from exposure to EMF and its damage. It cleans up negativity.

Galena is a strong protector against negative energies.

Hematite offers positive protection from EMF and is an excellent choice to place near your electronics.

Pyrite is a super protector from EMF. Use it in your place of work. In your home place it near your computers, microwave, and TV.

Lepidolite cleans out blockages created by EMF. Wear it as jewelry, in a pocket, or under a pillow.

Shungite is a strong crystal that fully absorbs negative energy that is especially generated by EMF. Place several places throughout your home.

Rose Quartz is excellent for clearing any space of EMF. Place pieces even in our automobile.

To summarize, here is what is what is known about EMF: Tissue heating can occur by holding your phone directly against your ear. Keeping earbuds in the ears for long periods of time. EMF can interfere with melatonin production and cause sleep disruption. It is recommended that you do not place a router in your bedroom. Some research has suggested that long-term exposure to EMF may cause cancer. More research is required to substantiate that. There are efforts to reduce exposure to EMF. Among these efforts are the following:

WI-FI Routers are now using beamforming technologies that focus the signals directly on connected devices, thus reducing the amount of radiation.

Manufacturers of cell phones are experimenting with ways to reduce radio frequency output without losing signal strength.

New appliances with an Energy Star rating have lower EMF emissions.

As you replace or buy new appliances and other electronic equipment keep in mind the SAR (Specific Absorption Rate). Be aware. Check things out.

ACTIVITY 15

Checking it Out

Take a few minutes, a walk through your home or office, and make a list of those items that you can shut down to reduce EMF, for example, consider disconnecting the following: printers, second television, extra electric clocks, equipment chargers.

SEVEN
HEALING YOURSELF VIBRATIONALLY

Sound is one of easiest ways to help in self-healing. This is especially true for sufferers of various allergies or who react negatively to medicinal drugs.

Sound vibration works on the physical body at the cellular level as well as the emotional level. And just maybe, it is the emotional level that should receive the most attention in today's world of pandemics, wars, threats of nuclear annihilation, prejudice, bigotry, and outright hatred, and environmental disasters of huge magnitude.

The busy and often hectic lives people lead, it is not always convenient or possible to have a personal sound treatment or a sound bath within a group setting. Giving yourself a sound treatment provides several benefits:

Reduction of personal stress.

Reduction of depression.

Improvement in sleep pattern.

Reduction in high blood pressure.

Reduction in energy blockages.

STRESS is one of the biggest threats to one's health. In addition to creating the development of significant disease patterns, it possesses the potentiality of creating mental issues in young children. It is unfortunate that stress has become an accepted part of everyday life. Stress can be controlled! Its negative impact can be reduced. Here is a simple first-line-of-defense: Humming. Humming has these benefits:

Significantly increases nasal nitric oxide a natural neural transmitter that is released as a gas while you breathe. It protects your body by sterilizing airborne pathogens.

Stimulates the vagus nerve that controls specific body functions such as your digestion, heart rate, and immune system.

Improves heart rate variability which is an indicator of how well you are to deal with stress.

ACTIVITY 16

A Little Hum Will Do You

Directions:

Select a favorite tune from your childhood, or a current song, or a simple sound such as *O.* To kick things up a notch, add some deep breathing as you home.

BHRAMARI PRANAYAMA

The practice of Bhramari Pranayama is from the Hindu Yoga practice of humming like the bees in a hive. The Sanskrit, Bhramari, means bee. It is also called the Humming Bee Breath. The buzzing sound that is created with this technique is meant to vibrate. You should feel it.

ACTIVITY 17

Just Do It

Sit in a comfortable yoga position or in a chair.

Next, keep your eyes closed.

Relax. Breathe naturally.

Place your hands on your head with your thumbs plugging your ears.

Your index fingers should be just above your eyebrows.

Middle fingers are above the eyelids,

Ring fingers above the upper lip

and the little fingers are below the lower lip.

See the illustration on the next page.

Take a deep breath through your nose, hold for the count of 5, and then push it out of the mouth and make the buzzing sound at the back of your throat. You should feel the vibration.

Concentrate on the buzzing sound. Do the exercise 10 times, 3 times a week.

BENEFITS:

Besides being useful in reducing stress, Bee Humming also improves sinus issues and hyperthyroidism.

A CAUTIONARY NOTE:

Some people go into a trance-like state doing this breathing exercise. When you are nearing the completion of the exercise, do not get up and start moving around. Take a few minutes before doing so. Returning to a normal state too quickly could cause some serious issues including dizziness and dysphoria. Move your hands, slowly move your legs and feet.

ACTIVITY 18

Getting It on in the Morning

This is an old recipe for relieving stress and beginning the day calmly. It will also stimulate your vagus nerve.

Directions:

Take a clean glass.

Fill it ¾ full of warm water.

Gargle with the water.

Depression the feeling of sadness and hopelessness that occur over long periods of time—months, even years. It is reflected as a lowered energy state and as a diminished life force. Unfortunately, depression is one of those conditions that may occur for no apparent reason or cause. Self-doubt, poor self-esteem, and a general malaise become one's daily companions. What needs to be understood is that it is chemical imbalance in the brain that is the chief cause of depression. Admittedly, the interactions of the brain's chemistry is not yet fully understood. What is known is that has something to do with the way neurochemicals are used by the brain. For example, two such neurochemicals that are well established are dopamine and serotonin.

The standard treatment for depression involves drugs. Despite the effectiveness of these drugs, there may be long- term negative impact on the over-all health of the sufferer. Sound vibration offers a drug-free app roach to dealing with depression. High-frequency sounds stimulates the left brain and provides a positive impact on the reduction of depression.

The 432Hz can help remove mental blocks and open a path to a more fulfilling life. The 432Hz is the frequency of Earth and nature. Connecting to this frequency relieves depression.

ACTIVITY 19

Tuning In

What You Will Need:

A set of Bluetooth headphones

iPad, laptop, cellphone, or computer

Copy this URL onto your devise:
https://pixabay.com/music/meditationspiritual-432-hz-music-for-healing-161531

Directions:

Sit in a comfortable recliner or other chair

Take 5 Ujjayi Breaths or Bee Breaths

Yawn

Play the URL and let the sound wash over you.

When the sound ends, stay still for a few minutes. Get up slowly, make sure you are steady on your feet before moving about.

Sleep, when continually disrupted by restless legs, aching muscles and joints, an over-active brain, and or nightmares the negative results are staggering: anxiety, stress, weight loos, anger, and frustration become common. Such an emotional rollercoaster creates erratic instability. Despite the many reports of immediate relief using sound therapy a stern warning is necessary. Vibration is not a panacea. It may take considerable time before genuine relief is experienced.

ACTIVITY 20

Diffuse It

<u>What You Will Need:</u>

A musical diffuser

1 cup distilled water (If not available, use tap water)

5 drops of Lavender Essential Oil

5 drops of Rosemary Essential One eyedropper

<u>Directions:</u>

Follow the direction that came with the diffuser when adding the water.

Add the essential oils

Select the music and play it just loud enough to be heard.

Turn on the diffuser just as you go to bed.

Take a few good breaths and gently exhale through the nose.

High Blood Pressure is a major issue. With 1, billion sufferers worldwide and at a cost of $100 billion dollars a year lifestyle changes are made using medication. These medications may bring about undesirable side effects such as dizziness, headaches, and dry mouth. One in ten cases, high blood pressure occurs because of underlying health issues. Among these are kidney disease, diabetes, underactive or overactive thyroid, and lupus.

Medicines that can create high blood pressure include contraceptive pills, steroids, cough and cold remedies, herbal remedies containing liquorice, and drugs such as cocaine and fentanyl.

World renowned Mayo Clinic has suggested ten lifestyle changes that can lower blood pressure. Among these suggestions are weight loss, exercise regularly, eat healthy, reduce salt intake, and stress. What else can one do to lower high blood pressure?

ACTIVITY 21

Beat It-Strike It

<u>What You Will Need:</u>

Handheld drum either a 16 inch or an 8-inch. Animal skin drums work very well. They do have a problem with too much or not enough humidity. This changes the sound.

A non-animal skin drum avoids the issue of humidity. The sound produced is excellent.

A large wooden spoon and a six-inch block of wood

Crystal bowl and striker

Steel Tongue Drum and striker

Directions for Drum:

You do not need to have any musical training. The goal is to create a steady monotonous sound.

Gently tap the drum with the drumstick along the lower outer edge of the drum. Slowly work your way to the center of the drum.

Drum for 10 minutes for the first three to five sessions per day

Add 5 minutes more. Do this for 1 to 2 weeks.

Check your blood pressure at the end of the session.

Directions for Wooden Spoon:

Place a block of wood on your desk or on a table.

Strike the block with a slow steady beat

Do this for 10 minutes when you first get up and just before retiring

Do this for two weeks and then check the blood pressure

Directions for Two Finger Drumming:

Use the first two fingers of your dominate hand. Tap the top of your desk. Do not tap so hard as to injury your fingers. Fancy it up just a bit by adding the first two fingers on your other hand. Do this for 3 or 5 minutes.

Directions for Crystal Bowls

Singing bowls are very popular in today's world of supportive healing medicine. The exact date of the origin of use of singing bowls is not known. Their existence is estimated to be around 560 BCE (Before Current Era) and are thought to have originated in the Himalayas, specifically in India and Nepal. From there, the use of singing bowls spread to China, Japan, Tibet, and the rest of the world.

The bowls are made of combination of various metals such as copper, iron, lead, gold and or silver. The use of the term "singing bowl" according to Srizu Bajracharya in "The Tale of the Singing Bowl" (published August 14, 2019 in the

Kathmandu Post) was coined by Jit Bahadur Shahi, a trader of handicrafts,"

There are many different types of singing bowls. Some of the well-recognized bowls include Naga, Lignan, Remuna, and Manu/Mudra. Bowl uses vary also and include bowls from which one may eat, storge for grain, begging, religious ceremonies, music, and healing.

During the 1980s singing bowls used for essential well-being moved into the public world and out of monasteries and temples. By 2000, therapists and healers of different backgrounds had firmly established private and group healing sessions with sound baths. Seven claimed benefits of using singing bowls include

Improved immunity

Improved blood pressure

Improved blood circulation

Increased mental awareness

Reduction of personal stress and anxiety

Reduction of pain

Reduction of depression

Singing bowls must be gently struck and rubbed to produce sound. Additionally, quality bowls with continue to resonate for several minutes after being struck.

There are several kinds of mallets or strikers used to create the melodious vibrations of a bowl. Each has a specific role. Among these mallets are the following popular types:

Crystal Mallet- One end is pure crystal while the other end is silicone or rubber
Fat Boy Mallet- Large round wooden stick covered in suede. Used with large crystal bowls
Gong Mallet- One end is large and is made of felt, wool, or rubber. A wooden handle is inserted in the gong. Generally used for large singing bowl rimming.
Wool Padded Mallet-Made of wood with one end covered in fine wool. Used to bring a bowl's frequencies into sync

Please note that different tones can be produced by different mallets as well as by different techniques.

Wah-wah technique is among the unique. It has been said that the name wah-wah comes from the late Jimi Hendrix's *Voodoo Child.* Whatever the origin of the term, it is an added oscillation to the sound created by a singing bowl that has that capability.

Rimming requires a padded mallet. Once the bowl's voice is clear, slow the movement of the mallet around the rim of the crystal bowl. **Striking** relies upon a padded mallet and is struck on the bowl's mid-exterior rim. I do not recommend striking the interior wall.

ACTIVITY 22

Bowling It Away

<u>Directions:</u>

Crystal bowls are popular and come in different sizes, colors, keys, and created for specific chakras.

Place the bowl of choice on a safe surface.

Gently strike the bowl on 3 sides, but not the one directly facing you

Once that has been done, run the mallet around the top edge of the bowl. Do this until the desired level of sound is produced. Let the sound play out.

Play the bowl for 10 minutes twice a day.

Energy Blockage refers to the interruption of the normal flow of energy in your body. It includes all living things. The sudden drop of energy can be indicative of something negative going on physically or emotionally. Individuals respond differently to energy blockages and treatment will vary. Blockages may be caused by physical trauma, serious illness, repressed emotional issues and or everyday stress.

We often forget that the five basic elements (ether, air, water, fire, and earth) forge a unity which provides us the sensations of form, taste, touch, smell, and sound. We also forget these elements come together inside of each of us and create energy. Our flow of energy is managed by what we call Chakras. The first five energy centers are located along the spine. The 7 main chakras and the symptoms of blockages are shown in the following chart:

CHAKRA LOCATION AND BLOCKAGE SYMPTOM

The Chakra	Location	Symptoms of Blockage
Root Chakra	Base of Spine	Fearful, depressed
Sacra Chakra	Reproductive organs	Emotional instability
Solar Plexus Chakra	Naval	Anger, unable to relax
Heart Chakra	Cardiac Region	Despair, Indifference
Throat Chakra	Throat	Frustration
Third Eye Chakra	Between Eyebrows	Confused, depressed
Crown Chakra	Just above the head	Mental confusion

Can an individual clear blocked energy or does one have to go to a shamanic healer? An individual can clear blocked energy. The first step is to locate the blockage. Here is a simple procedure you can do.

ACTIVITY 23

Location, Location

<u>What You Will Need</u>: (See Note)

One metal clothes hanger (preferably copper and no coating on the hanger

One pair of wire cutters

One pair of scissors

One clear plastic straw

<u>Directions:</u>

Cut the bottom wire from the rest of the hanger.

At 2 inches in from one end, bend the wire to for the letter L.

Cut a 2 to 2 ½ inch piece from the plastic straw

Insert the bent end of the wire into the small piece of straw.

Hold the "dowser" between your thumb and forefinger. Do not squeeze.

The dowser may move very rapidly and you do not want it to strike your face of eyes.

Move the dowser over your body.

Where it slows down or completely stops is the location of the energy blockage.

Once you have determined the location of the blockage do the following to help open the blockage so there an improved energy flow. Vibrational frequencies for essential oils range from 43Hz to 580Hz. It is generally agreed that disease begins at 58Hz. Human beings vibrate between 62-72Hz. This figure may vary depending on the individual. The following chart provides the MHz of the major organs of the human body.

NOTE: This activity has been presented in an earlier chapter. But because of its varied uses the author feels it is of value to repeat it. It marries well with the next activity.

ACTIVITY 24

Clearing the Way

Once you have the dowser made and have located an indicated blockage, the following will help you clear it away.

What You Will Need:

A small soft cloth pouch
5 crystals. (Clear Quartz, Amethyst, Citrine, Selenate, and Carnelian are suggested.)
Once you have the crystals, clean them with a soft damp cloth. Do not put the Selenite in water or use too much on the cloth to clean it. It will dissolve.
Your crystals now need to be charged. Place them in the sun for 3 to 5 hours.
Once the crystals have been charged, place them in the cloth bag.
Place the bag of crystals on the spot identified as to where the blockage is located. Do this for 20 minutes.
You may need to do these 3 or 4 times over a period of a couple of days.

ESSENTIAL OILS

It stands to reason that since essential oils have the highest vibrational frequency in the natural world, they would be very useful in clearing energy blockages. Humans vibrate between 62-72Hz. This still may vary depending on the individual. Essential oils have vibrational frequencies ranging from 42Hz to 580Hz. It stands to reason that essential oils have value in opening energy blockages. The following chart shows the MHz of 9 human organs.

Organ	MHz Range
Brain	71-90
Colon	50-60
Heart	67-70
Liver	55-60
Lungs	58-65
Pancreas	60-80
Stomach	58-65
Thymus	65-68
Thyroid	62-68

Using essential oils is an easy way to remove energy blockages. When you experience an energy blockage you may feel tired, physical pain, general physical or emotional discomfort, or have difficulty in getting things done. The following chart is a guide line to help you to choose an essential oil or oils to remove an energy blockage.

Even though there are more than 90 recognized essential oils not all are backed by research. These five popular essential oils have supporting research to back up claims for what they do: [vii]

Lemon Essential Oil-Enhances positive mood. (Olfactory Influence on mood, autonomic endocrine and immune function. PubMed April 2008)

Peppermint Essential Oil- Lessens fatigue and improves one's performance in exercising. (The effects of peppermint on exercise performance. PubMed March 2013

Rosemary Essential Oil- Enhances mood states and brain wave activity. (Effects of Inhaled

Rosemary Oil on Subjective Feelings and Activities of the Nervous System. NLM December 2012

Spearmint Essential Oil- When combined with Rosemary Essential Oil there is a benefit in learning and memory. Effects of Inhaled Rosemary Oil on Subjective Feelings and Activities of the Nervous System.

Sweet Orange Essential Oil can potentially improve athletic performance- Effects of Inhaled Rosemary Oil on Subjective Feelings and Activities of the Nervous System. September 22, 2016.

ACTIVITY 25

Oil It

What You Will Need:

Any two of the essential oils listed in the chart, Essential Oils Frequency Chart. If you have determined you have a heavy or strong blockage, use those oils with high megahertz.

A carrier oil such a Jojoba, Sweet Almond, or Olive Oil. If you have selected oils with a strong scent can tone it down by adding a less high megahertz oil and or increase the amount of carrier oil.

A dark colored bottle with stopper. The bottle should hold at least three ounces.

A teaspoon measuring spoon

Remember to do a patch test for using the oil mixture. If you find a redness around the spot of the patch test, stop using the oil and consult your medical doctor.

Directions:

Add 1 to 2 ounces of the carrier oil (Jojoba for example) to the bottle.

Add two drops of the chosen essential oils

Close the bottle, and gently shake it until the oils are well mixed.

Apply a couple of drops to the area of the blockage.

Do this once a day, preferably at bed time. Do this for three days.

Do a blockage test again. If you still have an issue, check with your medical doctor.

 ## ESSENTIAL OILS FREQUENCY CHART

OIL	FREQUENCY
BASIL	52 MHz
BLUE SPRUCE	520 MHz
FRANKINCENSE	147 MHz
GERMAN CHAMOMILE	105 MHz
HELICHYRSUM	181 MHz
JUNIPER	98 MHz
LAVENDER	118 MHz
MELISSA	102 MHz
MELROSE	48 MHz
MYRRH	103 MHz
PEPPERMINT	78 MHz
ROSE	320 MHz
ROSEMARY	320 MHz
SANDALWOOD	98 MHz

MHz stands for Megahertz

Copyright © 2023 Norman W. Wilson, Ph.D.

EIGHT
VIBRATIONAL FOODS

So far it has been implied, suggested, and methods named to help you increase your vibration to heal yourself. Among these have ben drums, crystal bowls, tuning forks. Singing and humming have had an immediate role to play in changing the human vibrational level. Recordings of Solfeggio Frequencies and other sounds have been discussed.

On area that is now getting considerable attention is the consumption of high vibrational foods. We are not talking about high energy drinks. But the idea of vibrational foods should not be a surprise since everything vibrates. In 1960, movie producer, Darryl Anka stated, "Ever thing is energy and that's all there is to it. Match the frequency of the reality you want and you cannot help but get that reality. It cannot be any other way." The question now is what are the high vibrational foods and what is their reality in transferring that vibrational energy to human beings?

There is no question about the foods we eat and their highly significant impact they have on our bodies—everything from our immune system, energy levels, heart health, sex drive, and yes, even our weight loss and or gain. Experience has taught that when things in our physical, mental, and emotional lives get out of balance, we suffer. Depending on the degree of being out of balance, we experience stress, despondency, and withdrawal from family and friends.

In addition to the use of sound vibration, one of the easiest ways to feel physically, mentally, and emotionally better is to eliminate low vibrational foods—specifically those foods that are highly processed. Commonly called "junk foods," these include most microwavable foods, foods with added sugar, fried foods, and certain cooking oils. Genetically Modified Organisms, trans fats, alcohol, and carbonated drinks should be added to the list.

The general recommendation, then, is to eat high vibration producing foods. High vibration foods include almost everything organic: Fresh vegetables as opposed to canned, leafy green vegetables, fresh fruits, herbs, nuts, and ancient grains. Free-range chickens, grass-fed cows, and wild fish belong on the list.

Note that according to Wikipedia, "Ancient Grains is a marketing term used to describe a category of grains and pseudocereals that are purposed to have been minimally changed by selective being over recent millennia, as opposed to more widespread cereals such as corn, rice, and modern varieties of wheat. Ancient grains are often marketed as more nutritious than modern grains, though their health benefits over modern verities have been disputed."

There is a list of foods called "The Dirty Dozen." These foods contain the most pesticides and agricultural chemicals. The following chart is based on Renee Onque's article.[viii]

THE DIRTY DOZEN FOOD GROUP

*NOTE: Greens include Kaye, Collards, and Mustard.

COPYRIGHT© 2023 NORMAN W. WILSON, Ph.D.

According to CNBC'S *Make It* report, dated March 29m 2023, "Nearly 75% of non-organic fresh produce sold in the United States contains residues of potentially harmful pesticides. The implication for human low energy is tremendous.

What then are the high vibrational foods? HFFs (High Frequencies Foods) are those foods that have not been processed, have no chemical added including sugars and salts, and have not undergone genetic modification. The vibrational frequency level of foods is determined by a vibrational spectroscopy. Check this URL for further information on spectroscopy: https://www.ncbi.nlm.nih.gov/pmc/articles/PMC8834424/

Functioning on a high vibrational level depends on several things: One's creative nature, personality, looking at the world with curiosity and awe, daring to dream, one's physical well-being, and the consumption of high frequency-vibrational foods. The following illustrated chart, based on the lists created by Dr. Marcus Ettinger[ix] shows the five high vibrational food categories.

5 HIGH FREQUENCY - VIBRATIONAL FOODS
(ORGANIC)

1. Dark leafy greens and green juice
Land versions
Green vegetables contain chlorophyll, plant blood, which absorbs sunlight - energy. Leafy greens, like spinach, collards, kale, dandelion greens, Brussels sprouts, zucchini, broccoli, and bok choy vibrate at high frequencies. These greens are high in alkaline minerals, which balance acidity, assist in proper waste elimination, and retard disease.

Water versions
Sea vegetables — arame, dulse, hijiki, nori, Pacific or Atlantic kelp, bladderwrack (type O blood)
Algae (blue-green; Klamath Lake [fresh water], spirulina [salt water]) Algae (green; chlorella).

2. Tropical fruit (ripe)
Mango, papaya, pineapple, and carambola aka starfruit. These are more or less edible versions of sunshine.

3. Sprouts
Sprouted seeds (including nuts, grains, legumes, and beans) are loaded with vitamins, minerals, phytonutrients, and enzymes, as well as highly digestible forms of complete protein.
1. Plants, baby (sprouted) — buckwheat grass, fava bean greens, pea tendrils, sunflower sprouts, sweet potato greens, and wheatgrass.
2. Sprouts (light by weight) and green sprouts — alfalfa, broccoli, chia, clover, garlic, onion, and radish.
3. Seeds (sprouted) — flax, hemp, pumpkin, sesame, and sunflower.

4. Raw Cacao (Raw Chocolate)
While humans have to work hard to produce enough anandamide to reach higher levels of ecstasy, only one plant produces this chemical as part of its normal metabolism, **Cacao**! Not only does cacao contain anandamide in high concentrations. When we eat *raw cacao*, the anandamide produced by our brains along with the anandamide found in cacao may continue to circulate in the body for extended periods of time, helping us feel great all day long.

5. Medicinal Mushrooms
All edible mushrooms resonate with high vibrational energy, but Chaga and Reishi possess the highest vibrational energy, in my opinion. Medicinal mushrooms possess immune-modulating, antioxidant, and anti-inflammatory properties. Reishi, like raw cacao, increases "shen." Shen is the life-force energy you have in abundance when the heart is in balance. Shen gives you passion, enthusiasm, confidence, purpose, and vision. However, it also gives you patience, good judgment, perspective, humility, and sobriety. The more shen one possess the more ethereal he or she becomes.

What does organic food mean? According to the US Department of Agriculture a product is considered organic if it is certified *to have grown on soil that had no prohibited substances applied for three years* prior to harvest. What then, are the prohibited substances? These substances include synthetic chemicals, pesticides, and in terms of animal food, no antibiotics, hormones, or GMO.

If these items are no longer added to the growing processes why then, is this 294-billion dollar a year business still so expensive? Here is a summary of the five-point explanation of the reason for the high price:

Supply is limited compared to demand

Production costs are higher

Mandatory segregation of organic and conventional produce

Distribution costs are higher, and Inspection fees farmers pay are higher

Even though it appears organics are the recipients of more attention does not mean or imply that "conventionally" grown food and raised chicken and cows are of little value nutritionally and economically. Whichever you choose, organic and traditional grown vegetables, both must be thoroughly washed before eating. Spraying the fruit and vegetables with Lavender Hydrosol and then rinsing them is a good practice to follow. The following chart shows additional high vibrational foods and what the contribute to one's health.

ADDITIONAL HIGH VIBRATIONAL FOODS AND WHAT THEY HELP DO

FOOD	WHAT IT DOES
Blueberries	Lowers blood pressure
Mangoes	Prevents weight gain
Sprouts	Folate rich
Garlic	Reduces LDL Cholesterol
Cinnamon	Reduces Inflammation
Turmeric	Nutrient for the brain
Nuts	High in protein & fiber
Chia Seeds	Omega-3 fatty acids
Matcha	Heart & Brain health
Kefir	Microflora of the gut
Mushrooms*	Mental focus
Saurkraut	Aids digestion
Pineapple	Anti-inflammatory
Medjool Dates	High fiber

Overcooking, leaving unrefrigerated, and keeping too long lessens the nutritional value of all vegetables and fruits.

*Medicinal Mushrooms include Lion's Maine, Turkey Tail, Chaga, Lingzi, and Oyster Mushrooms.

NINE
THE CHAKRAS HAVE IT

Millions of words have rolled off the press that define, explore, and explain chakras. To add that mass would appear to be repetitive. Yet there is an area that should be explored: Vibration and its impact on the chakras.

As a brief review it can be said that a chakra is a center point of energy in the human body. Oops! That's not quite right. Animals as well as the Earth itself have chakra points or centers. But, let's begin with the human being and its body.

The Ancient Indian Vedic literature says the human body has 7 chakras and each has a color, function, and location.

Crown Chakra—White or Violet color, located at the top of the head, spirituality, and higher consciousness

Third Eye Chakra—Indigo color, located on the forehead between the eye brows, intuition, foresight, and inner wisdom

Throat Chakra—Blue color, clarity and truth, mind and heart are aligned

Heart Chakra— Green color, located around the center of the chest, involves two specific types of issues: physical health and emotional health

Solar Plexus Chakra—Yellow color, Located in the upper abdomen, personal power, and self-esteem

Sacral Chakra—Orange color, located just below one's navel, regulates creativity, emotional expression, and sexuality

Root Chakra—Red color, located at the base of the spine, stability and security, survival instincts and basic human needs.

The following chart, *The 7 Chakras*, provides the Indian name of the chakras.

Chart is from Just Some Yoga.com

The 7 chakras can become blocked. Following is a list of the signs that a chakra is blocked.

BLOCKED CHAKRAS

Blocked chakras mean there is a lack of sufficient flow of energy to maintain your mental, physical, and emotional health.

Crown Chakra that is blocked shows up as chronic headaches, neurological issues, confusion, a sense of being lost or an emotional crisis.

Third Eye Chakra that is blocked is indicated by a lack of clarity, poor decision-making, headaches, or vision issues.

Throat Chakra blockage is indicated by difficulty in expressing your thoughts, feeling misunderstood, sore throat, and or thyroid problems.

Heart Chakra blockage may show up as bitterness, lung issues, jealousy, heart issues, as a sense of being abandonment. Relationships may become difficult to maintain.

Solar Plexus Chakra blockage is indicated by digestive problems, lack of self-control, a sense of being overwhelmed, low self-esteem, and feeling helpless.

Sacral Chakra blockage shows up as a disconnect with relationships, emotions, creativity, sexual dysfunction.

Root Chakra blockage has the following symptoms: anxiety, bowl issues, back pain, fear, insecurity, and possessiveness.

UNBLOCKING THE CHAKRAS

There are things you can personally do to unblock chakras.

Meditate regularly. Include mindfulness practices

Claim a quiet time each day

Visualizing a violet light just above the top of your head.

Use essential oils in a diffuser, especially Frankincense (See the section of Diffusers and Recipes)

Do a 20-minute yoga session

Eat root vegetables

Become involved in creative activities

Do deep breathing exercises

USING SOUND TO HEAL CHAKRAS

It has nearly become an old 'saw" that everything vibrates and vibration creates sound and that sound heals. To say that sound heals not only the physical but also the emotional and mental issues. All of that pales when you realize sound vibration resonates with the soul.

Each of the seven chakras gets energized or re-charged by specific musical notations. The following musical notes and their matching chakras are shown in the following chart. They are based on 432Hz.[x]

MUSICAL NOTE	CHAKRA
C	Root
D	Sacral
E	Solar Plexus
F	Heart
G	Throat
A	Third Eye
B	Crown

Millions of people suffer stomach issues. The musical notation of E helps to recharge the 3rd Chakra, the Solar Plexus

Singing Tibetan Bowls, Crysal Bowls are available to match those musical notations. Drums, flutes, rattles, and other sound producing instruments are helpful. Often it comes down to personal choice.

THE VOICE AS A HEALING INSTRUMENT

It is reasonably safe to say the human voice was humankind's first instrument of sound. It can be solo, with a partner, or group. For a voice master in using healing voice sounds check the works of Jonathan Goldman.

ACTIVITY 26

Singing Along

What You Will Need:

A yoga matt

A yoga pillow

A comfortable chair

Directions:

Sit in the yoga position on a mat

Or on a yoga pillow. Be comfortable. Be sure to sit with your back straight

Sit in a chair in which you will be comfortable and can keep your back straight.

Take 5 deep breaths and exhale slowly

As you exhale, say AAAEE AA—H

Elongate the sound. Do this for ten minutes.

ACTIVITY 27

Just the Two of You

<u>What You Will Need:</u>

Another person

A double yoga matt

<u>Directions:</u>

Sit facing each other

Touch your hands (If you are comfortable, hold hands)

Take 5 deep breaths, exhaling slowly

Sing OM as you try to match pitch.

Note if may take a few practices to match the pitch.

TEN
HEALING ANIMALS' CHAKRAS

As do humans, animals have chakras. These spots of energy vortices traditionally called Petals flow along an auric meridian system into the physical body. This energy flows in and out in cats and dogs as it does in human beings. Whatever the stimuli ism it leaves it mark in the aura and impacts the physical and emotional life of the cat or dog. Different color vibration are emitted by animal chakras and is nearly the same as in humans. The difference is the alignment of the chakras. In cats and dogs, the chakra positions are horizontal *instead of vertical.*

Like humans, animals have an *Etheric Chakra System*. And most animals have 8 major chakras, up to 21 minor chakras and 6 smaller energy points called *Bud Chakras*. These are the animals 4 paw pads, and a bud of skin at the opening of ach ear. There is a chakra unique to animals; an extra one in addition to the 8. It the *Brachial or Key Chakra*.

The chakras can be stimulated for training and or healing purposes. The location of the animal chakras is shown in the following charts:

ANIMAL CHAKRAS' LOCATIONS

CHAKRA	COLOR	LOCATION
Root	Red	Base of tail
Sacral	Orange	Lower Belly*
Solar Plexus	Yellow	Upper Chest**
Heart	Green	Heart Area
Throat	Blue	Upper Throat
Brachia	Black	Shoulders
Brow	Indigo	Between Eyes***
Crown	Violet	Top of Head

*Just above the sex organs

**A few inches from the front legs

*** In humans the Third Eye

ANIMAL CHAKRAS' LOCATIONS ILLUSTRATED

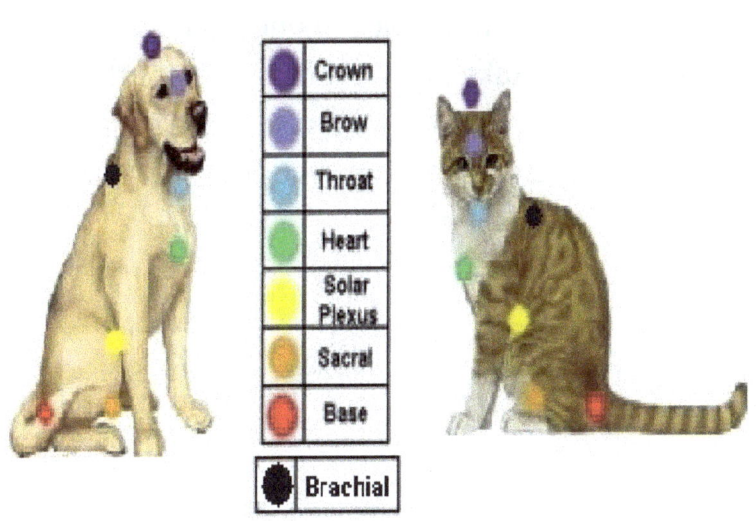

Animal Chakra Points

Illustration from Naturalchakrahealing.com Specifically "Animal Chakras and Energy Centers"

Animals as well as humans show signs when the chakras are out of balance. It takes a bit of practice to identify the signals that indicate an imbalance and potential health issues. The following chart shows some of the potential symptoms a cat or dog may show when it is experiencing an imbalance in one or more of their chakras. It will take some practice to note the symptoms. The following chart lists the chakras and the issues or symptoms your pet may show.

SYMPTOMS OF CHAKRA IMBALANCE

CHAKRA	SYMPTOM
Root	Fearful, sluggish, restless
Sacral	Whinny and mewing
Solar Plexus	Aggressive, dominating
Heart	Dejected, jealous, sad
Throat	Very noisy, won't obey
Brow	Distant, distracted,
Crown	Depression, withdrawn
Brachial	Doesn't want to be touched, inflamed skin

ACTIVITY 28

The Tender Touch

Before attempting to check your pet's chakras there is some necessary preparation.

Bring yourself into a healing state of mind. You can do this by the following:
Meditate for 15 minutes before examining your pet. Softly hum the OM sound, or do a 5- to 10-minute-deep breathing exercise

Wash your hands and dry them. Consider using Lavender Hydrosol. Then, massage your hands to bring about a full blood flow.

You are now ready to take the necessary steps to locate the blocked chakras. If you do not wish to use your hands use the EMF Detector.

Show the tool to your pet. Give it time to sniff it. Lay it on the pet's back. It needs to learn that it is not a danger.

If you choose to use your hands, place your hands or four fingers on each hand about 2 inches above the chakra for small animals and 2 to 4 inches for larger animals. This may vary due to your vibrational sensitivity.

If you feel a small or slight vibration or a subtle warmth that indicates no blockage. If, on the other hand, you feel nothing, take a minute, and gently rub your hands together.

Then either lay your hands on the chakra or keep them just above the chakra. Keep your hands in that position for several minutes. Repeat in 2 hours.

If you do not notice a positive change, call your Veterinarian.

This is a modified Reiki treatment.

CHAKRA TUNING

Each chakras has a specific sound vibration. Knowing the sound and its vibration allows you to break the blockage that may be causing your pet discomfort.

The following chart includes the hertz and the vocal sound to use with each chakra.

CHAKRA, HERTZ, AND VOCAL SOUND

Chakra	Hertz	Vocal Sound
Root	256	Uh
Sacral	288	Ooh
Solar Plexus	320	Oh
Heart	341.	Ah
Throat	384	Eye
Brow	448	Aye
Crown	480	Eee
Brachial	10kHz	Om

ACTIVITY 29

Singing Along

Place your dominate hand on the animal's chakra and make the vocal sound for that chakra. Holding the vocal sound may take some practice. Do that for ten minutes.

In addition to the human voice recorded sounds can be used to heal a blocked chakra and this is especially true for Solfeggio Sounds. (See Chapter Four) Each chakra has a solfeggio hertz to which it responds.

CHAKRA	SOLFEGGIO HERTZ
Root	396Hz
Sacral	417Hz
Solar Plexus	528Hz
Heart	639Hz
Throat	741Hz
Brow	852Hz
Crown	963Hz
Brachial	10KHz*

ACTIVITY 30

Boom, Boom It

What You Will Need:

A mini ultra slim Bluetooth speaker that works with an iPhone, iPad, laptop, or PC

A recording of Solfeggio sounds

Directions:

Place the speaker near the cat or dog's blocked chakra. Underneath the pet's bed or pillow.

Play the Solfeggio for 10 minutes, twice a day for 5 days. Do not play it loud. Soft, quiet. Animal ears are very sensitive.

If there is no improvement contact your veterinarian.

Another way to help the healing processes of the animals' chakras is to add crystals to the treatment regimen. Each of the major chakras may have more than one associated crystal.

ACTIVITY 31

What You Will Need:

Three crystals for the blocked chakra, i.e. 3 rubies.

A small cloth bag that can be tied

Directions:

Clean the crystals in temped water and dry with a soft cloth

Place the 3 crystals in the sunlight for 3 to 5 hours, depending on the amount of sunlight available.

Add the 3 crystals to the cloth bag, tie it.

Place the bag near the pet's blocked chakra, preferably under the pet's bed or blanket. Leave it there for a week Again, if you do not see an improvement, contact your veterinarian.

There is controversy over the use of essential oils and the treatment of dogs and cats. It appears that much of the issue is caused by the direct application of an essential oil to the animal. Anymore than one does to humans, do not apply essential oils that are not mixed with a carrier oil directly to the skin. Those essential oils that are deemed safe to use with pets include the following and the chakra to which they may be used:

ESSENTIAL OIL	**CHAKRA**
Cedarwood	Root
Turmeric	Sacral
Lemon	Solar Plexus
Copaiba	Heart
Arborvitae	Throat
Petitgrain	Brow
Frankincense	Crown
Lavender	Brachial

Before moving into Activity 32, there are at least a dozen essential oils that should never be used on cats. Among these are Basil, Bergamot, Birch, Cinnamon, Clove, Dill, Fennel, Tea Tree, Oregano, Peppermint, Rosemary, and Thyme.

ACTIVITY 32

What You Will Need:

>The oil of choice for the blocked chakra
>A 4-inch piece of cotton cloth or three cotton balls.
>An eye dropper
>Carrier oil such as jojoba

Directions:

>Mix 5 drops of the essential oil with 15 drops of the carrier oil
>Soak the cloth or cotton balls with the oil
>Place under the pet's bed or blanket
>Leave it for 3 days. Discard
>Wait 3 days, repeat.

Check regularly each day to make sure your cat is not experiencing any negative reaction. If any signs appear, immediately stop using the treatment, clean the cat's bed, and contact your veterinarian.

If you have concerns about that degree of exposure to an essential oil, placing 5 drops in a diffuser is an acceptable substitute. Place the diffuser in the room where the cat beds down for the night.

Remember, these activities are not substitutes for medical treatment and are offered only as suggested support.

Bibliography for vibrational healing:

Books:

Gerber, R. (2001). Vibrational Medicine: The #1 Handbook of Subtle-Energy Therapies. Bear & Company.

Eden, D., & Feinstein, D. (1999). Energy Medicine: Balancing Your Body's Energies for Optimal Health, Joy, and Vitality. Penguin.

Dale, C. (2000). The Subtle Body: An Encyclopedia of Your Energetic Anatomy. Sounds True.

Tiller, W. A. (1997). Science and Human Transformation: Subtle Energies, Intentionality and Consciousness. Pavior Publishing.

Rappaport, J. (2009). Vibrational Healing: Revealing the Essence of Nature through Aromatherapy and Essential Oils. North Atlantic Books.

Gerber, R. (2001). Vibrational Medicine for the 21st Century: The Complete Guide to Energy Healing and Spiritual Transformation. Piatkus Books.

Abrams, A. (2001). Vibrational Healing Through the Chakras: With Light, Color, Sound, Crystals, and Aromatherapy. Crossing Press.

Articles and Journals:

Oschman, J. L. (2000). Energy Medicine: The Scientific Basis. Churchill Livingstone.

Thompson, W. L. (2004). The Role of Energy Medicine in the Future of Healthcare. Alternative Therapies in Health and Medicine, 10(6), 48-56.

Rubik, B. (2002). The Biofield Hypothesis: Its Biophysical Basis and Role in Medicine. Journal of Alternative and Complementary Medicine, 8(6), 703-717.

Benor, D. J. (2001). Spiritual Healing: A Unifying Influence in Complementary

Therapies. Journal of Alternative and Complementary Medicine, 7(4), 337-340.

Gerber, R. (1995). Vibrational Medicine Comes of Age. Journal of Holistic Nursing, 13(1), 77-89.

Recent studies on the use of vibration to heal

As of January 2022, there have been ongoing studies and research on the use of vibration for healing purposes. While I can't provide information on very recent studies beyond that date, I can give you an overview of some areas where vibration therapy has been researched and its potential applications:

Bone Healing and Osteoporosis: Vibration therapy has been studied for its potential in promoting bone health and accelerating fracture healing. Research has shown promising results in improving bone density and strength, particularly in individuals with osteoporosis or those at risk of bone fractures.

Musculoskeletal Rehabilitation: Vibration therapy is being explored as a modality for musculoskeletal rehabilitation, including its use in reducing muscle soreness, improving flexibility, and enhancing muscle strength and power. This is particularly relevant for athletes and individuals undergoing physical therapy.

Pain Management: Studies have investigated the use of vibration therapy for managing various types of pain, including chronic lower back pain, neuropathic pain, and musculoskeletal pain. The mechanisms by which vibration may alleviate pain include modulation of pain signals and activation of sensory nerves.

Balance and Mobility: Vibration therapy has been researched for its effects on balance and mobility, especially in older adults and individuals with neurological conditions such as Parkinson's disease or stroke. Vibrational platforms and devices are being studied as potential interventions to improve balance control and reduce the risk of falls.

Wound Healing: Some studies have explored the use of low-frequency vibration therapy for enhancing wound healing, particularly in chronic wounds such as diabetic ulcers. Vibration may stimulate cellular activity, improve blood circulation, and promote tissue regeneration, leading to faster wound closure.

Neurological Conditions: There is ongoing research into the use of vibration therapy for neurological conditions such as multiple sclerosis, spinal cord injury, and cerebral palsy. Vibration may have neuroprotective effects and could potentially help improve motor function and sensory perception in these populations.

Mental Health and Well-being: While less studied, there is some research suggesting that vibration therapy may have beneficial effects on mental health and well-being. Vibration-induced relaxation and stress reduction have been reported in some studies, although more research is needed in this area.

These are just a few examples of the research areas related to vibration therapy for healing purposes.

Also, By Norman W Wilson, PhD

Available at Fiction4All.com, and other online retailers

Dr. Wilson's

Courses Available on UDEMY.com

Healing-The Shaman's Way

Healing-The Shaman's Way Using Crystals

Healing-The Shaman's Way Using Herbs

Healing-The Shaman's Way Using Essential Oils

Healing-The Shaman's Way Using Vibration to Heal

Check YouTube for Dr. Wilson's videos.

ENDNOTES

[i] Tuning the Human Biofield. Healing with Vibrational Sound Therapy. Rochester. Healing Arts Press. 2014. P.32

[ii] Exploring Vibration Therapy: Definition, Uses, and Key Benefits. January 1, 2024. Hue Light USA. Longevity Care System.

[iii] https://www.youtube.com/watch?v=C2EMPO0BYJI

[iv] A popular song composed by Dutch lyrists, Peter Koelewijn.

[v] Some sources provide a slightly different Hertz for the brain wave state. For example: Alpha Waves are given as 8 to 14 Hertz and Gamma Waves 30 to 100 Hertz.

[vi] A 2018 study from Japan indicates 528Hz significantly reduced stress in the endocrine system and the autonomic nervous system. More astonishing is the indication that 528Hz

[vii] Based on Healthline August 2019.

[viii] 2023's 'Dirty Dozen': The 12 Fruits and Vegetables with the most Pesticides—and 4 tips for enjoying them safely. CNBC. Make it. Health and Wellness. March 29, 2023.

[ix] Ettinger, Marcus. High Frequency- Vibrational Food Groups for Health and Increased Consciousness. August 29, 2016. Advanced Healing.

[x] This chart is based on one designed by D. Geetanjali Jha, Head of Cyberpsychology Research at iMature EdTech. "Fractal Enlightenment Healing Your Chakras with Music and Vibrations. Nov. 7, 2016.

www.ingramcontent.com/pod-product-compliance
Lightning Source LLC
Chambersburg PA
CBHW070458100426
42743CB00010B/1669